THIS PLANNER BELONGS TO:

Name: ………………………………………………

SUCCESSFUL PRODUCTPRENEUR AT:

Business: ………………………………………....

"You Don't Have To Get It Perfect....
You Just Have To Get It Going!"

About Catherine
& the Productpreneur Academy

Hi, I'm Catherine Langman, founder of the Productpreneur Academy.

It's not in my nature to settle for 'the way things have always been done'.

And I'm betting, seeing as you're holding this planner, you don't either.

Because that's why you're in business, right? To sell your product, which is undoubtedly a much better, more innovative, more effective solution to an age-old problem than anything else on the market.

I'm a business coach, marketing consultant, teacher, blogger and...

My genius is teaching business owners how to plan for growth, how to get their products in the hands of more people, and how to become a household brand (whilst stressing less, working smarter and enjoying yourself as much as possible!).

But what on earth is a Productpreneur? You might ask...

Because making up words is fun, I call those of us who design or invent their own product inventions, build their own brands, and create a business in order to sell them, PRODUCTPRENEURS.

I "get" Productpreneurs – I understand what makes them tick and what drives their business. Because I am one – a successful one – and since selling my first business I've had numerous Productpreneurs approach me, wanting to learn what my secret sauce was...

Like many good things in life, I became a Productpreneur almost by accident.

Back in 2005, I became a mother. My first son was a honeymoon baby and boy what a life-changer he was! I thought being a Mum (that's Australian for Mom if you're playing along from the other side of the globe) was the best thing since sliced bread – so good in fact that I had another son a year later.

There was absolutely no way I could go back to my previous career after that. My background was in branding and advertising for blue chip corporate and government clients (the Coca Colas and Microsofts of the world).

But the ethical dilemma of designing packaging for a tobacco company and the boredom of creating advertising for a bank drove me to seek a more professionally satisfying and family-friendly role.

So I started my business. But I wasn't just creating a job for myself – I was on a mission to change the world, one nappy (or diaper!) at a time.

Inspired by my own baby, my business designed, manufactured, distributed and retailed eco-friendly nappies for babies.

I wanted to create a business that was lucrative, successful, and yet flexible around the needs of my family.

And that's exactly what I did.

I went on to create one of the first eco-friendly nappy brands to hit the big time, leading the brand from a small eBay-only presence to one stocked in retailers nationally and exporting globally (from New Zealand, to Asia, Dubai, UK, Europe and the United States.)

One of the biggest accolades I received during this time was the Telstra Business Awards, which is like the Academy Awards for privately owned businesses in Australia! What a thrill to be recognised by some very illustrious high achievers!

Along the way, I grew my business from a micro operation run from my dining room table into a highly profitable business, consistently doing 5-6 figures each month in sales.

How did I achieve this?

By creating a repeatable system for online sales as well as robust wholesale distribution. AND by building a brand that truly connected with my audience.

My unique process, tailored to those who are commercialising their own invention and building their own brand, allows you to get your brand noticed as well as to grow an army of raving fans both online and offline.

Sound enticing?

If you've already got the product and you need help with building the brand and the business around it, I can show you how.

Let's do this!

How To Use This Planner

Before you get started using this Marketing Planner, I want you to think about something really important:

How would you describe 'success' in your business?

Is it a profitable lifestyle business?

An empire?

Or perhaps a fully automated passive income stream?

You need to be clear about what success looks like for YOU. Because it will be different for everyone, and it's not my business to tell you what yours should be…

I'll walk you through a process to help you to articulate what your big business vision looks like.

I'll show you how to diagnose what issues and opportunities exist that you really want to act on.

And then I'll help you to figure out exactly what strategies you want to focus on implementing in your business.

But even more importantly, I give you a system for tracking your progress. So you will ALWAYS stay focused on the tasks that matter most.

This is the single most important factor in success! I cannot emphasize that enough.

Without further ado - I invite you to get cracking!

Catherine x

Your Business Vision

Several years ago I was a judge for the AusMumpreneur of the Year Business Awards, tasked with helping to decide who would take out the biggest award for the year.

The finalists for this big award were all extremely savvy and successful business women. As you can imagine, the calibre of entrants was very high.

The stories these women told, about the *spark of inspiration* that started their business, the *hurdles they've had to jump* through and hard lessons learned, the *key decisions* they made that lead to their success, and their *big visions* for their business and their personal lives, were all so incredibly inspiring!

After listening to all the finalists' presentations, it was absolutely clear that there was **one key factor** that was common across all their success stories:

They all had a huge goal, a really big vision for their business.

And actually, digging even a little bit deeper, all of these business superstars had three sides to their big goal: **passion, purpose and profit.**

Take Monica of Whole Kids for example. She started her business out of a passion for feeding kids wholesome, healthy food, something that was inspired by a trip to Indonesia years ago working with children in poverty.

Her goal for her business is to serve 50 million healthy kids meals! No small feat. She also supports three children's charities and is committed to environmental sustainability (and has been awarded B-Corp certification for her efforts).

In the last decade she has grown an internationally-recognised, multi-million dollar company that continues to grow by over 40% each year!

Monica was not alone amongst the awards finalists for her ambitious goals and commitment to her purpose, but her outstanding successes did earn her the title of AusMumpreneur of the Year award.

Let's take a leaf out of these successful business women's playbook and create a Big Vision for your business.

Specifically: what would you do in your business if you couldn't fail?

Describe that vision on the next page.

Describe your vision...

Knowing Your Customers Like They're Your Best Friend

The first step in growing your sales online is: **customer clarity.** Why? Well, the truth is that customer-centric businesses tend to have most success with selling online. In the anonymous online world, the business that has the best, most natural product/customer fit, wins!

Here are the top three reasons why truly, deeply and madly understanding your customers helps you to sell more products online:

> Your **copywriting** gets better because you'll start using the right words, the same words and phrases your ideal customers use.

> Your website **content** will be more effective, because you will know when (in your customers' decision-making process) to deliver the right information and the right offers, and via which medium.

> You will attract **more potential customers** because you know where your audience is and how to speak to them.

When you fully understand your ideal customer, your business will really start to make more money. You'll stop wasting your time and effort trying to be all things to all people. Which, quite frankly, is pretty annoying when you're on the receiving end of it!

The end result? All your messaging – from your website, to emails, blogs and social media – will have more impact and your customers will learn to know, like and trust you. And when you're selling online, that is pure gold.

Use the following template to profile your ideal customer.

I call it a **Customer Avatar**, but it is also sometimes known as **Customer Persona** or **Buyer Profile.**

Your Customer Avatar is a detailed description of your ideal customer's personality, needs, desires, aspirations, values, beliefs, problems, and so on, as it relates to your product and brand. You may have one really clear buyer profile, or you may have more than one.

If you have more than one distinct customer profile, then choose one to be your primary one (this would be the largest 'group' and who you would tailor your content and marketing messages to), and then subsequent customer profiles would be secondary to that.

Keep this Persona handy each time you create new content in your business, whether it be for social media, emails, advertising, your website or even in-person content like in-store or trade shows. Remember, consistency is key!

AVATAR NAME:

SHORT DESCRIPTION:

QUOTE:

AGE:

GENDER:

MARITAL STATUS:

& AGE OF CHILDREN:

LIVES / LOCATION:

FAVOURITE BOOKS OR
MAGAZINES:

FAVOURITE BLOGS OR
WEBSITES:

FAVOURITE TV SHOWS:

FAVOURITE INSTAGRAM
PROFILES:

INDUSTRY LEADERS OR
ASSOCIATIONS:

DESIRES /
ASPIRATIONS:

VALUES / BELIEFS:

PAIN POINTS / NEEDS /
STRUGGLES:

WHAT WOULD STOP
YOUR CUSTOMER FROM
BUYING?:

WHAT DOES YOUR
CUSTOMER NEED TO
BELIEVE TO OVERCOME
OBJECTIONS TO BUY?:

Discover Your Unique Selling Proposition

A unique selling proposition (USP) is what makes your business stand out from the crowd and tells your customers what is special about you. So, as a brand owner, it's vital to get it right.

We're always reading about how many messages customers are bombarded with every day. They cannot re-evaluate services and products every time they need to make a purchase. That would simply be too time consuming!

So, to make life easier, we tend to organise products and services into groups and position them accordingly. For instance, the *safest car*, the *most expensive* car or the *best value* car.

Here's a worksheet to help you identify your own USP and use it to help your ideal customers connect with your business and brand.

List the top 3 attributes your ideal customer looks for.

1.

2.

3.

Identify 3 of your top competitors.

1.

2.

3.

What are these competitors most known for? (ie what is their USP?)

Competitor 1:

Competitor 2:

Competitor 3:

Now for the fun part! List the top 3 things that makes YOUR brand stand out.

What gives your brand a competitive advantage?

1.

2.

3.

Rank your 'stand out' factors on a scale of 1-10 (10 being the best) based on what your customer would be most drawn to.

Lastly, write a brief USP statement.

Explain what makes your brand different and better than your competition, and why your customers respond to your brand and product.

For example, Warby Parker's is as follows:

"Warby Parker was founded with a rebellious spirit and a lofty objective: to offer designer eyewear at a revolutionary price, while leading the way for socially conscious businesses."

Year In Review

Look back before you can plan ahead

Before you put pen to paper with your business plan, you want to review your past year's performance.

I know this can be a bit tedious, and sometimes also a bit scary if you're still in the early stages of your business and not turning a profit yet!

(Take heart – everyone starts like this, but with a good plan you'll be able to get ahead!)

Here are some questions to guide your review:

What were your biggest business accomplishments from the past year?

What were some of the lessons you learned or challenges from the past year?

What were the weak points? What do you think needs to improve?

Were there any missed opportunities in the last 12 months?

Were there any ways to improve customer service?

Did any areas of the business feel disjointed or 'out of whack'?

What marketing worked this year? What created wins?

If there was one word that describes your past year, what would that be?

Time to SWOT

You can complete this exercise even if you're brand new in business and don't have any previous historical data to analyse.

Have you ever done a SWOT analysis? (Or am I now talking Greek to you?!)

SWOT stands for Strengths, Weaknesses, Opportunities and Threats.

Basically, you want to get real with yourself here. No kidding yourself about how things really are.

Strengths and Weaknesses relate to your own personal abilities and that of your team. They are INTERNAL to the business.

Are you fantastic at social media marketing, but suck at writing emails? Or brilliant at driving sales, but your order fulfilment or customer service really lags behind?

Opportunities and Threats relate to what's going on in your industry.

Are there any new competitors coming to market? Or have you identified a fantastic new product opportunity that you reckon would be absolutely killer?

Your Thoughts...

Your turn - time to SWOT!

STRENGTHS

What are the current strengths of the business?

WEAKNESSES

What are the current weaknesses of the business?

What are your current personal strengths?

What are your current personal weaknesses (this may lead to possibly outsourcing things you're doing in-house but really shouldn't)?

OPPORTUNITIES

What are your BIGGEST
opportunities in the next year?

THREATS

Are there any threats to the
business itself?

What are you most excited about?

Are there any threats to the market
/ industry / product category?

Know Your Numbers

When it comes to running a product business, whether you have an eCommerce business or you're a brand selling wholesale or export, there are certain numbers or metrics that you need to know.

The metrics you want to look at are things like the number of leads (prospective customers) you're getting, your conversion rate (the proportion of leads converted to customers) and revenue.

All these numbers are indicators of your success or progress in your business.

Here are the metrics you want to track weekly, monthly and annually.

eCommerce

Total Weekly Revenue

Conversion Rate

# of Conversions (Orders)

Average Order Value

Website Visitors (Unique)

% New Visitors

Abandoned Cart Rate

Bounce Rate

Email Subscribers

New Subscribers Added to List

Open Rate

Click Through Rate

I also like to track the proportion of total weekly revenue attributed to each individual marketing channel (such as organic search, social media, email marketing, paid search, and so on).

Refer to the templates later in this Planner to help you track your numbers.

Wholesale / export

Total weekly revenue

Total number of wholesale / export stockists

Average order value

Repeat order frequency

new stores contacted (leads)

Conversion rate of leads to new stockists

Your Thoughts...

Annual Metrics Review Worksheet

Next, dig into your website reports, your accounts, your Paypal, and your Google analytics, to find out exactly where you are right now.

How much revenue did you make in the last 12 months? (Actual vs goal/budget)

How much did you grow from the previous year?

How profitable were you? List gross profit before expenses, and net after expenses.

What is your current average order value?

How many website visitors do you get each month?

What is your current website conversion rate?

If you wholesale - how many stockists do you have?

What is your repeat customer rate?

How many email subscribers do you have right now?

Value-Based Pricing

The two most common pricing strategies I see with Productpreneurs are:

> "Cost Plus Margin" (pricing products by adding a profit margin on top of the cost of goods), and

> "Competitor Based" (essentially looking around at your competitors and pricing yourself within a similar range).

I agree that both these methods seem quite logical.

But the problem with both options is: neither of them convey anything about the quality of your products.

And customers will ALWAYS make a value judgement based on your price.

I always advocate against pricing products on the cheap end of the scale. Being a low-cost product may make *you* feel better about yourself and like you're not 'ripping off your customers'.

But being the cheapest product actually only attracts customers who don't place a very high value on what you sell.

Whereas - price your product based on the perceived value your customers place on it, and you'll be a whole lot more profitable.

Remember - your product range plus service combined is what makes up the value you provide to your customers.

So even if you sell the same or similar products to competitors, but you have more expertise or better or faster service, your customers will perceive your business to offer more value.

On the next page you'll see an exercise to help you work out your pricing.

And finally - you do want to track your sales every week. You'll find space for that further on in this planner.

Pricing for Profits

If you're making or manufacturing your own products, make sure you include the cost of materials, labour, packaging, shipping and customs costs into your Cost per Unit.

If you wholesale, I typically double the unit cost and add an extra 10-12% to reach the wholesale price.

The retail price is typically double the wholesale price, although this varies somewhat in different product categories.

PRODUCT NAME	UNIT COST	WHOLE-SALE PRICE	WHOLE-SALE MARGIN	RETAIL PRICE	RETAIL MARGIN

How Will You Know
If Your Campaign Worked?

Reviewing your past marketing campaigns determines your success just as much as planning your next ones.

Measuring and analysing your campaign results can provide unique insight into your audience, marketing channels, and budget.

It can also tell you exactly how (or how not) to run your next campaign.

So before you decide what marketing strategies, promotions, product launches or offers you will run over the next 12 months, let's take a look at your results from your past major campaigns or promotions.

Start with your goals

Did your previous campaign or promotion achieve your revenue goals? If it did - great! If it didn't, it can still be considered a success.

For example, if your goal was to increase website visitors by 100K, any bump in traffic would be considered successful.

But there's a difference in a campaign that works and a campaign that's worthwhile. A worthwhile campaign gives you an ROI that's proportionate to the time and energy you put into it.

While it's okay to celebrate any bump in traffic and sales, don't assume that's enough.

There's a reason the very first thing to do is set a campaign goal. Sticking to that goal and calibrating your investment will ensure your campaign is worthwhile.

Review all the metrics

This step helps maximise your campaign's impact. When you analyse results and apply those insights to your future marketing, its value increases tenfold.

Not only did it help you measure and assess your campaign results, but it'll also give you direction and clarity on your audience, marketing methods, creative prowess, and more.

Use the worksheet on the next page to analyse your campaign results.

What insights can you learn?

Ask yourselves questions like:

What went so well that we would do it again?

What could've been done differently?

How could we have saved money?

For anything that went wrong, why do we think it went wrong?

What did we learn about our audience or marketing channels?

Your Thoughts...

Annual Review of Major Campaigns

What was the campaign name / theme / product / offer?

What were the objectives or goals for the campaign?

Review the creative / design / imagery - were you happy with it? Did customers love it?

How much did you spend on advertising? (Separated per channel)

How many new customers did you acquire?

Did you increase repeat purchase rate?

How many orders did you receive? (Separate per channel)

What was the average order value and total revenue generated?

Did you add new email subscribers to your list?

How many website visitors did you have?

What was your cost per website visitor?

What was your cost per email subscriber?

What was your cost per new customer acquired?

What was your revenue per website visitor?

What was your revenue per email subscriber?

What was your revenue per customer?

What was the ROI (return on investment) per channel?

"How do you eat an elephant? One bite at a time..."

Goal Setting for the Year Ahead

Today we're going to start with a method for setting goals to help drive your business forward. Here's how…

Think big (but not too big!)
It's important to set ourselves big, challenging goals.

A big goal motivates us to work harder and this stretches our potential.

A small goal might be easily attainable, but once we achieve those easy goals we're much less likely to keep pushing ourselves to improve or grow further than that. So we don't achieve nearly as much.

So think big - but not so far out of the realms of possibility that you completely set yourself up to fail!

(For example - it would be silly of me to set myself the goal of becoming an Olympic marathon runner, when I can barely run 2km without falling off the treadmill!)

Have a think about:
What would you do in your business in the next year if you couldn't fail?

How much revenue do you want to make? What % growth does this represent?

What products do you want to sell? What customers do you want to serve?

Do you want to be featured on prime time TV? Or stocked in a big box retailer?

Big tip:
When thinking about your annual goals - make sure they are a logical stepping stone towards achieving your Big Vision.

Next:
Use the worksheet on the next page to figure out how to translate your big goal into smaller goals for each quarter, month, week and day.

Goal Setting Worksheet

Planning to the now:

This planning strategy is adapted from Gary Keller's "The ONE Thing" (which if you haven't already read, you should get onto it - it's life changing for the entrepreneur!)

Big Vision / BHAG (Big Hairy Audacious Goal)
What's the one big goal you want to achieve?

Five-Year Goal
Based on your Someday (BHAG) goal, what do you need to achieve
in 5 years to be on track?

One-Year Goal
Based on your Five-Year goal, what do you need to achieve this year to be on track?

Monthly Goal
Based on your One-Year goal, what do you need to achieve this month to be on track?

Weekly Goal
Based on your Monthly goal, what do you need to achieve this week to be on track?

The Growth Strategy Matrix

A growing business is able to do two things very effectively:

Grow an audience to attract potential new customers, and

Convert new and repeat sales.

Without a constant stream of potential customers, and a mechanism to convert them into buyers (preferably who buy more than once), then you don't have a business.

So you need to include a mix of strategies in your marketing plan that achieves both.

Let's take a look at the Growth Strategy Matrix:

Strategy 1:

Sell new products to new customers

Strategy 2:

Sell more of your existing products to new customers

Strategy 3:

Sell new products to your existing customers

Strategy 4:

Sell more of your existing products to your existing customers

Strategies to build your audience

When it comes to selling new or existing products to new customers, then firstly you must implement audience-building and awareness-building strategies.

To grow your audience, you need to figure out a way to connect with groups of your ideal customers. The best way to do this is to tap into other existing audiences.

You can do this through:

PR / publicity

Work with Influencers or Brand Reps

Paid advertising in traditional or digital media

Trade shows or Expos

Strategic partnerships or collaborations with other brands

Search engine optimisation

Strategies to convert more sales

When it comes to converting more sales, you want to think about the different sorts of customers you might have in your audience.

Generally you'll have some customers who always want what's new and will pay full price. Some are likely to be high dollar value customers who buy large amounts at once. And some will be your bargain hunters and tend to only buy on sale.

So you want to consider strategies like:

regular promotions

new products

special offers

Bundles

And use marketing channels such as social media, paid advertising, and email marketing (both broadcast and automated funnels) to convert the sales.

Next: Use the Growth Matrix worksheet on the next page to plan your growth strategies for this year.

Choose Your Growth Strategies

Use the grid below to plan out the strategies you will employ to build your audience and convert more sales.

Strategy 1: Sell new products to new customers

Strategy 2: Sell more of your existing products to new customers

Strategy 3: Sell new products to your existing customers

Strategy 4: Sell more of your existing products to your existing customers

Quarterly Goals Planner

Once you have decided on your annual goals, which should be measurable and time limited, your next step is to figure out what you need to do each quarter in order to reach your annual goal.

QUARTER 1	QUARTER 2
1.	1.
2.	2.
3.	3.
4.	4.
5.	5.

KPIS / OUTCOMES	KPIS / OUTCOMES
1.	1.
2.	2.
3.	3.

Use this quarterly planner to allocate strategies you will implement and the expected outcomes you anticipate achieving for each quarter. For example, a strategy might be to launch a new product using email marketing, Facebook advertising and exhibiting at a trade show. The expected outcomes might include a revenue number and repeat customer rate, plus the number of new email list subscribers and website visitors.

QUARTER 3

1.

2.

3.

4.

5.

QUARTER 4

1.

2.

3.

4.

5.

KPIS / OUTCOMES

1.

2.

3.

KPIS / OUTCOMES

1.

2.

3.

Monthly Action Planner

What do you want to complete or achieve this month? Take the time to plan out the tasks or actions you need to complete in order to successfully implement each strategy listed in your Quarterly Goals Planner.

Month:

TASKS	WEEK 1	WEEK 2	WEEK 3	WEEK 4

TASKS	WEEK 1	WEEK 2	WEEK 3	WEEK 4

Monthly Content Planner

Month:

	EMAIL NEWSLETTER TOPIC/OFFER:	BLOG TOPIC/OFFER:
WEEK 1:		
WEEK 2:		
WEEK 3:		
WEEK 4:		

Themes

FACEBOOK: INSTAGRAM: PINTEREST: YOUTUBE:

Month: 1 2 3 4 5 6 7 8 9 10 11 12

WEEK	MONDAY	TUESDAY	WEDNESDAY
THIS WEEK'S PRIORITIES			
THIS WEEK I WANT TO…			

WORK/BUSINESS TO-DOS

THURSDAY	FRIDAY	SAT/SUN	WEEK IN REVIEW
			WINS
			REVENUE
			NUMBER OF ORDERS
			AVERAGE ORDER VALUE
			WEBSITE VISITORS/ LEADS
PERSONAL TO-DOS			CONVERSION RATE
			NEXT WEEK

Month: 1 2 3 4 5 6 7 8 9 10 11 12

WEEK	MONDAY	TUESDAY	WEDNESDAY
THIS WEEK'S PRIORITIES			
THIS WEEK I WANT TO...			

WORK/BUSINESS TO-DOS

THURSDAY	FRIDAY	SAT/SUN	WEEK IN REVIEW
			WINS
			REVENUE
			NUMBER OF ORDERS
			AVERAGE ORDER VALUE
			WEBSITE VISITORS/ LEADS
PERSONAL TO-DOS			CONVERSION RATE
			NEXT WEEK

Month: 1 2 3 4 5 6 7 8 9 10 11 12

WEEK	MONDAY	TUESDAY	WEDNESDAY
THIS WEEK'S PRIORITIES			

THIS WEEK I WANT TO…

WORK/BUSINESS TO-DOS

THURSDAY	FRIDAY	SAT/SUN	WEEK IN REVIEW
			WINS
			REVENUE
			NUMBER OF ORDERS
			AVERAGE ORDER VALUE
			WEBSITE VISITORS/ LEADS
PERSONAL TO-DOS			CONVERSION RATE
			NEXT WEEK

Month: 1   2   3   4   5   6   7   8   9   10   11   12

WEEK	MONDAY	TUESDAY	WEDNESDAY
THIS WEEK'S PRIORITIES			
THIS WEEK I WANT TO…			
WORK/BUSINESS TO-DOS			

THURSDAY	FRIDAY	SAT/SUN	WEEK IN REVIEW
			WINS
			REVENUE
			NUMBER OF ORDERS
			AVERAGE ORDER VALUE
			WEBSITE VISITORS/ LEADS
PERSONAL TO-DOS			CONVERSION RATE
			NEXT WEEK

The monthly metrics

Website

OF VISITORS

OF ORDERS

$ OF SALES

CONVERSION RATE

OF NEW VISITORS

% BOUNCE RATE

FB Ads

OF VISITORS

OF ORDERS

$ OF SALES

CONVERSION RATE

ROAS

TOTAL SPEND

Emails

EMAILS SENT

OPEN RATE

OF ORDERS

$ OF SALES

CONVERSION RAT

Social Media

OF VISITORS

OF ORDERS

$ OF SALES

CONVERSION RATE

Other

OF VISITORS

OF ORDERS

$ OF SALES

CONVERSION RATE

MONTHLY SALES GOAL

MONTHLY SALES ACHIEVED

DIFFERENCE

What worked well this month

What didn't work well this month

Special occurrences during the month
(Ie Black Friday, Mother's Day, school holidays, product launch etc)

Monthly Action Planner

What do you want to complete or achieve this month? Take the time to plan out the tasks or actions you need to complete in order to successfully implement each strategy listed in your Quarterly Goals Planner.

Month:

TASKS	WEEK 1	WEEK 2	WEEK 3	WEEK 4

TASKS	WEEK 1	WEEK 2	WEEK 3	WEEK 4

Monthly Content Planner

Month:

	EMAIL NEWSLETTER TOPIC/OFFER:	BLOG TOPIC/OFFER:
WEEK 1:		
WEEK 2:		
WEEK 3:		
WEEK 4:		

Themes

FACEBOOK: INSTAGRAM: PINTEREST: YOUTUBE:

Month: 1 2 3 4 5 6 7 8 9 10 11 12

WEEK	MONDAY	TUESDAY	WEDNESDAY
THIS WEEK'S PRIORITIES			
THIS WEEK I WANT TO...			

WORK/BUSINESS TO-DOS

THURSDAY	FRIDAY	SAT/SUN	WEEK IN REVIEW
			WINS
			REVENUE
			NUMBER OF ORDERS
			AVERAGE ORDER VALUE
			WEBSITE VISITORS/ LEADS
PERSONAL TO-DOS			CONVERSION RATE
			NEXT WEEK

Month: 1 2 3 4 5 6 7 8 9 10 11 12

WEEK	MONDAY	TUESDAY	WEDNESDAY
THIS WEEK'S PRIORITIES			
THIS WEEK I WANT TO…			

WORK/BUSINESS TO-DOS

THURSDAY	FRIDAY	SAT/SUN	WEEK IN REVIEW
			WINS
			REVENUE
			NUMBER OF ORDERS
			AVERAGE ORDER VALUE
			WEBSITE VISITORS/ LEADS
PERSONAL TO-DOS			CONVERSION RATE
			NEXT WEEK

Month: 1 2 3 4 5 6 7 8 9 10 11 12

WEEK	MONDAY	TUESDAY	WEDNESDAY
THIS WEEK'S PRIORITIES			

THIS WEEK I WANT TO…

WORK/BUSINESS TO-DOS

THURSDAY	FRIDAY	SAT/SUN	WEEK IN REVIEW
			WINS
			REVENUE
			NUMBER OF ORDERS
			AVERAGE ORDER VALUE
			WEBSITE VISITORS/ LEADS
PERSONAL TO-DOS			CONVERSION RATE
			NEXT WEEK

Month: 1 2 3 4 5 6 7 8 9 10 11 12

WEEK	MONDAY	TUESDAY	WEDNESDAY
THIS WEEK'S PRIORITIES			
THIS WEEK I WANT TO...			
WORK/BUSINESS TO-DOS			

THURSDAY	FRIDAY	SAT/SUN	WEEK IN REVIEW
			WINS
			REVENUE
			NUMBER OF ORDERS
			AVERAGE ORDER VALUE
			WEBSITE VISITORS/ LEADS
PERSONAL TO-DOS			CONVERSION RATE
			NEXT WEEK

The monthly metrics

Website

OF VISITORS

OF ORDERS

$ OF SALES

CONVERSION RATE

OF NEW VISITORS

% BOUNCE RATE

FB Ads

OF VISITORS

OF ORDERS

$ OF SALES

CONVERSION RATE

ROAS

TOTAL SPEND

Emails

EMAILS SENT

OPEN RATE

OF ORDERS

$ OF SALES

CONVERSION RAT

Social Media

OF VISITORS

OF ORDERS

$ OF SALES

CONVERSION RATE

Other

OF VISITORS

OF ORDERS

$ OF SALES

CONVERSION RATE

MONTHLY SALES GOAL

MONTHLY SALES ACHIEVED

DIFFERENCE

What worked well this month

What didn't work well this month

Special occurrences during the month
(Ie Black Friday, Mother's Day, school holidays, product launch etc)

Monthly Action Planner

What do you want to complete or achieve this month? Take the time to plan out the tasks or actions you need to complete in order to successfully implement each strategy listed in your Quarterly Goals Planner.

Month:

TASKS	WEEK 1	WEEK 2	WEEK 3	WEEK 4

TASKS	WEEK 1	WEEK 2	WEEK 3	WEEK 4

Monthly Content Planner

Month:

	EMAIL NEWSLETTER TOPIC/OFFER:	BLOG TOPIC/OFFER:
WEEK 1:		
WEEK 2:		
WEEK 3:		
WEEK 4:		

Themes

FACEBOOK: INSTAGRAM: PINTEREST: YOUTUBE:

Month: 1 2 3 4 5 6 7 8 9 10 11 12

WEEK	MONDAY	TUESDAY	WEDNESDAY
THIS WEEK'S PRIORITIES			
THIS WEEK I WANT TO…			

WORK/BUSINESS TO-DOS

THURSDAY	FRIDAY	SAT/SUN	WEEK IN REVIEW
			WINS
			REVENUE
			NUMBER OF ORDERS
			AVERAGE ORDER VALUE
			WEBSITE VISITORS/ LEADS
PERSONAL TO-DOS			CONVERSION RATE
			NEXT WEEK

Month: 1 2 3 4 5 6 7 8 9 10 11 12

WEEK	MONDAY	TUESDAY	WEDNESDAY
THIS WEEK'S PRIORITIES			

THIS WEEK I WANT TO...

WORK/BUSINESS TO-DOS

THURSDAY	FRIDAY	SAT/SUN	WEEK IN REVIEW
			WINS
			REVENUE
			NUMBER OF ORDERS
			AVERAGE ORDER VALUE
			WEBSITE VISITORS/ LEADS
PERSONAL TO-DOS			CONVERSION RATE
			NEXT WEEK

Month: 1 2 3 4 5 6 7 8 9 10 11 12

WEEK	MONDAY	TUESDAY	WEDNESDAY
THIS WEEK'S PRIORITIES			
THIS WEEK I WANT TO...			

WORK/BUSINESS TO-DOS

THURSDAY	FRIDAY	SAT/SUN	WEEK IN REVIEW
			WINS
			REVENUE
			NUMBER OF ORDERS
			AVERAGE ORDER VALUE
			WEBSITE VISITORS/ LEADS
PERSONAL TO-DOS			CONVERSION RATE
			NEXT WEEK

Month: 1 2 3 4 5 6 7 8 9 10 11 12

WEEK	MONDAY	TUESDAY	WEDNESDAY
THIS WEEK'S PRIORITIES			

THIS WEEK I WANT TO…

WORK/BUSINESS TO-DOS

THURSDAY	FRIDAY	SAT/SUN	WEEK IN REVIEW
			WINS
			REVENUE
			NUMBER OF ORDERS
			AVERAGE ORDER VALUE
			WEBSITE VISITORS/ LEADS
PERSONAL TO-DOS			CONVERSION RATE
			NEXT WEEK

The monthly metrics

Website

OF VISITORS

OF ORDERS

$ OF SALES

CONVERSION RATE

OF NEW VISITORS

% BOUNCE RATE

FB Ads

OF VISITORS

OF ORDERS

$ OF SALES

CONVERSION RATE

ROAS

TOTAL SPEND

Emails

EMAILS SENT

OPEN RATE

OF ORDERS

$ OF SALES

CONVERSION RAT

Social Media

OF VISITORS

OF ORDERS

$ OF SALES

CONVERSION RATE

Other

OF VISITORS

OF ORDERS

$ OF SALES

CONVERSION RATE

MONTHLY SALES GOAL

MONTHLY SALES ACHIEVED

DIFFERENCE

What worked well this month

What didn't work well this month

Special occurrences during the month
(Ie Black Friday, Mother's Day, school holidays, product launch etc)

Quarterly Goal Review

If there was one thing you could do to significantly increase your chances of successfully achieving your goals, would you do it?

Yes? Great! Because here it is: **Take the time every 90 days to review your progress.**

QUARTERLY GOAL 1:

What was your goal?

Did you achieve it? Y/N

Write down your results (good or bad):

What was the difference in actual vs goal?

What actions or events contributed to these results?

How does this affect your annual goal?

What would you do again or do diferently next time?

QUARTERLY GOAL 2:

What was your goal?

Did you achieve it? Y/N

Write down your results (good or bad):

What was the difference in actual vs goal?

What actions or events contributed to these results?

How does this affect your annual goal?

What would you do again or do diferently next time?

By monitoring and reviewing your progress, you will see how much you've achieved already, and this can have a powerful psychological impact on how motivated and positive you feel. Give yourself an hour to review your goals using the following worksheet as a guide.

Go back to the goals you made for the Year and the Quarter and enter them here to see how you are tracking.

QUARTERLY GOAL 3:	QUARTERLY GOAL 4:
What was your goal?	What was your goal?
Did you achieve it? Y/N	Did you achieve it? Y/N
Write down your results (good or bad):	Write down your results (good or bad):
What was the difference in actual vs goal?	What was the difference in actual vs goal?
What actions or events contributed to these results?	What actions or events contributed to these results?
How does this affect your annual goal?	How does this affect your annual goal?
What would you do again or do diferently next time?	What would you do again or do diferently next time?

Monthly Action Planner

What do you want to complete or achieve this month? Take the time to plan out the tasks or actions you need to complete in order to successfully implement each strategy listed in your Quarterly Goals Planner.

Month:

TASKS	WEEK 1	WEEK 2	WEEK 3	WEEK 4

TASKS	WEEK 1	WEEK 2	WEEK 3	WEEK 4

Monthly Content Planner

Month:

	EMAIL NEWSLETTER TOPIC/OFFER:	BLOG TOPIC/OFFER:
WEEK 1:		
WEEK 2:		
WEEK 3:		
WEEK 4:		

Themes

FACEBOOK: INSTAGRAM: PINTEREST: YOUTUBE:

Month: 1 2 3 4 5 6 7 8 9 10 11 12

WEEK	MONDAY	TUESDAY	WEDNESDAY
THIS WEEK'S PRIORITIES			
THIS WEEK I WANT TO…			

WORK/BUSINESS TO-DOS

THURSDAY	FRIDAY	SAT/SUN	WEEK IN REVIEW
			WINS
			REVENUE
			NUMBER OF ORDERS
			AVERAGE ORDER VALUE
			WEBSITE VISITORS/ LEADS
PERSONAL TO-DOS			CONVERSION RATE
			NEXT WEEK

Month: 1 2 3 4 5 6 7 8 9 10 11 12

WEEK	MONDAY	TUESDAY	WEDNESDAY
THIS WEEK'S PRIORITIES			
THIS WEEK I WANT TO…			

WORK/BUSINESS TO-DOS

THURSDAY	FRIDAY	SAT/SUN	WEEK IN REVIEW
			WINS
			REVENUE
			NUMBER OF ORDERS
			AVERAGE ORDER VALUE
			WEBSITE VISITORS/ LEADS
PERSONAL TO-DOS			CONVERSION RATE
			NEXT WEEK

Month: 1 2 3 4 5 6 7 8 9 10 11 12

WEEK	MONDAY	TUESDAY	WEDNESDAY
THIS WEEK'S PRIORITIES			
THIS WEEK I WANT TO…			

WORK/BUSINESS TO-DOS

THURSDAY	FRIDAY	SAT/SUN	WEEK IN REVIEW
			WINS
			REVENUE
			NUMBER OF ORDERS
			AVERAGE ORDER VALUE
			WEBSITE VISITORS/ LEADS
PERSONAL TO-DOS			CONVERSION RATE
			NEXT WEEK

Month: 1 2 3 4 5 6 7 8 9 10 11 12

WEEK	MONDAY	TUESDAY	WEDNESDAY
THIS WEEK'S PRIORITIES			
THIS WEEK I WANT TO…			
WORK/BUSINESS TO-DOS			

THURSDAY	FRIDAY	SAT/SUN	WEEK IN REVIEW
			WINS
			REVENUE
			NUMBER OF ORDERS
			AVERAGE ORDER VALUE
			WEBSITE VISITORS/ LEADS
PERSONAL TO-DOS			CONVERSION RATE
			NEXT WEEK

The monthly metrics

Website

OF VISITORS

OF ORDERS

$ OF SALES

CONVERSION RATE

OF NEW VISITORS

% BOUNCE RATE

FB Ads

OF VISITORS

OF ORDERS

$ OF SALES

CONVERSION RATE

ROAS

TOTAL SPEND

Emails

EMAILS SENT

OPEN RATE

OF ORDERS

$ OF SALES

CONVERSION RAT

Social Media

OF VISITORS

OF ORDERS

$ OF SALES

CONVERSION RATE

Other

OF VISITORS

OF ORDERS

$ OF SALES

CONVERSION RATE

MONTHLY SALES GOAL

MONTHLY SALES ACHIEVED

DIFFERENCE

What worked well this month

What didn't work well this month

Special occurrences during the month
(Ie Black Friday, Mother's Day, school holidays, product launch etc)

Monthly Action Planner

What do you want to complete or achieve this month? Take the time to plan out the tasks or actions you need to complete in order to successfully implement each strategy listed in your Quarterly Goals Planner.

Month:

TASKS	WEEK 1	WEEK 2	WEEK 3	WEEK 4

TASKS	WEEK 1	WEEK 2	WEEK 3	WEEK 4

Monthly Content Planner

Month:

	EMAIL NEWSLETTER TOPIC/OFFER:	BLOG TOPIC/OFFER:
WEEK 1:		
WEEK 2:		
WEEK 3:		
WEEK 4:		

Themes

FACEBOOK: INSTAGRAM: PINTEREST: YOUTUBE:

Month: 1 2 3 4 5 6 7 8 9 10 11 12

WEEK	MONDAY	TUESDAY	WEDNESDAY

THIS WEEK'S
PRIORITIES

THIS WEEK I WANT
TO…

WORK/BUSINESS TO-DOS

THURSDAY	FRIDAY	SAT/SUN	WEEK IN REVIEW
			WINS
			REVENUE
			NUMBER OF ORDERS
			AVERAGE ORDER VALUE
			WEBSITE VISITORS/ LEADS
PERSONAL TO-DOS			CONVERSION RATE
			NEXT WEEK

Month: 1 2 3 4 5 6 7 8 9 10 11 12

WEEK	MONDAY	TUESDAY	WEDNESDAY
THIS WEEK'S PRIORITIES			

THIS WEEK I WANT TO...

WORK/BUSINESS TO-DOS

THURSDAY	FRIDAY	SAT/SUN	WEEK IN REVIEW
			WINS
			REVENUE
			NUMBER OF ORDERS
			AVERAGE ORDER VALUE
			WEBSITE VISITORS/ LEADS
PERSONAL TO-DOS			CONVERSION RATE
			NEXT WEEK

Month: 1 2 3 4 5 6 7 8 9 10 11 12

WEEK	MONDAY	TUESDAY	WEDNESDAY
THIS WEEK'S PRIORITIES			
THIS WEEK I WANT TO…			

WORK/BUSINESS TO-DOS

THURSDAY	FRIDAY	SAT/SUN	WEEK IN REVIEW
			WINS
			REVENUE
			NUMBER OF ORDERS
			AVERAGE ORDER VALUE
			WEBSITE VISITORS/ LEADS
PERSONAL TO-DOS			CONVERSION RATE
			NEXT WEEK

Month: 1 2 3 4 5 6 7 8 9 10 11 12

WEEK	MONDAY	TUESDAY	WEDNESDAY
THIS WEEK'S PRIORITIES			
THIS WEEK I WANT TO…			
WORK/BUSINESS TO-DOS			

THURSDAY	FRIDAY	SAT/SUN	WEEK IN REVIEW
			WINS
			REVENUE
			NUMBER OF ORDERS
			AVERAGE ORDER VALUE
			WEBSITE VISITORS/ LEADS

PERSONAL TO-DOS			CONVERSION RATE
			NEXT WEEK

The monthly metrics

Website

OF VISITORS

OF ORDERS

$ OF SALES

CONVERSION RATE

OF NEW VISITORS

% BOUNCE RATE

FB Ads

OF VISITORS

OF ORDERS

$ OF SALES

CONVERSION RATE

ROAS

TOTAL SPEND

Emails

EMAILS SENT

OPEN RATE

OF ORDERS

$ OF SALES

CONVERSION RAT

Social Media

OF VISITORS

OF ORDERS

$ OF SALES

CONVERSION RATE

Other

OF VISITORS

OF ORDERS

$ OF SALES

CONVERSION RATE

MONTHLY SALES GOAL

MONTHLY SALES ACHIEVED

DIFFERENCE

What worked well this month

What didn't work well this month

Special occurrences during the month
(Ie Black Friday, Mother's Day, school holidays, product launch etc)

Monthly Action Planner

What do you want to complete or achieve this month? Take the time to plan out the tasks or actions you need to complete in order to successfully implement each strategy listed in your Quarterly Goals Planner.

Month:

TASKS	WEEK 1	WEEK 2	WEEK 3	WEEK 4

TASKS	WEEK 1	WEEK 2	WEEK 3	WEEK 4

Monthly Content Planner

Month:

	EMAIL NEWSLETTER TOPIC/OFFER:	BLOG TOPIC/OFFER:
WEEK 1:		
WEEK 2:		
WEEK 3:		
WEEK 4:		

Themes

FACEBOOK: INSTAGRAM: PINTEREST: YOUTUBE:

Month: 1 2 3 4 5 6 7 8 9 10 11 12

WEEK	MONDAY	TUESDAY	WEDNESDAY
THIS WEEK'S PRIORITIES			
THIS WEEK I WANT TO…			
WORK/BUSINESS TO-DOS			

THURSDAY	FRIDAY	SAT/SUN	WEEK IN REVIEW
			WINS
			REVENUE
			NUMBER OF ORDERS
			AVERAGE ORDER VALUE
			WEBSITE VISITORS/ LEADS
PERSONAL TO-DOS			CONVERSION RATE
			NEXT WEEK

Month: 1 2 3 4 5 6 7 8 9 10 11 12

WEEK	MONDAY	TUESDAY	WEDNESDAY
THIS WEEK'S PRIORITIES			
THIS WEEK I WANT TO...			
WORK/BUSINESS TO-DOS			

THURSDAY	FRIDAY	SAT/SUN	WEEK IN REVIEW
			WINS
			REVENUE
			NUMBER OF ORDERS
			AVERAGE ORDER VALUE
			WEBSITE VISITORS/ LEADS
PERSONAL TO-DOS			CONVERSION RATE
			NEXT WEEK

Month: 1 2 3 4 5 6 7 8 9 10 11 12

WEEK	MONDAY	TUESDAY	WEDNESDAY
THIS WEEK'S PRIORITIES			
THIS WEEK I WANT TO…			
WORK/BUSINESS TO-DOS			

THURSDAY	FRIDAY	SAT/SUN	WEEK IN REVIEW
			WINS
			REVENUE
			NUMBER OF ORDERS
			AVERAGE ORDER VALUE
			WEBSITE VISITORS/ LEADS
PERSONAL TO-DOS			CONVERSION RATE
			NEXT WEEK

Month: 1 2 3 4 5 6 7 8 9 10 11 12

WEEK	MONDAY	TUESDAY	WEDNESDAY
THIS WEEK'S PRIORITIES			

THIS WEEK I WANT TO…

WORK/BUSINESS TO-DOS

THURSDAY	FRIDAY	SAT/SUN	WEEK IN REVIEW
			WINS
			REVENUE
			NUMBER OF ORDERS
			AVERAGE ORDER VALUE
			WEBSITE VISITORS/ LEADS
PERSONAL TO-DOS			CONVERSION RATE
			NEXT WEEK

The monthly metrics

Website

OF VISITORS

OF ORDERS

$ OF SALES

CONVERSION RATE

OF NEW VISITORS

% BOUNCE RATE

FB Ads

OF VISITORS

OF ORDERS

$ OF SALES

CONVERSION RATE

ROAS

TOTAL SPEND

Emails

EMAILS SENT

OPEN RATE

OF ORDERS

$ OF SALES

CONVERSION RAT

Social Media

OF VISITORS

OF ORDERS

$ OF SALES

CONVERSION RATE

Other

OF VISITORS

OF ORDERS

$ OF SALES

CONVERSION RATE

MONTHLY SALES GOAL

MONTHLY SALES ACHIEVED

DIFFERENCE

What worked well this month

What didn't work well this month

Special occurrences during the month
(Ie Black Friday, Mother's Day, school holidays, product launch etc)

Quarterly Goal Review

If there was one thing you could do to significantly increase your chances of successfully achieving your goals, would you do it?

Yes? Great! Because here it is: **Take the time every 90 days to review your progress.**

QUARTERLY GOAL 1:

What was your goal?

Did you achieve it? Y/N

Write down your results (good or bad):

What was the difference in actual vs goal?

What actions or events contributed to these results?

How does this affect your annual goal?

What would you do again or do diferently next time?

QUARTERLY GOAL 2:

What was your goal?

Did you achieve it? Y/N

Write down your results (good or bad):

What was the difference in actual vs goal?

What actions or events contributed to these results?

How does this affect your annual goal?

What would you do again or do diferently next time?

By monitoring and reviewing your progress, you will see how much you've achieved already, and this can have a powerful psychological impact on how motivated and positive you feel. Give yourself an hour to review your goals using the following worksheet as a guide.

Go back to the goals you made for the Year and the Quarter and enter them here to see how you are tracking.

QUARTERLY GOAL 3:	QUARTERLY GOAL 4:
What was your goal?	What was your goal?
Did you achieve it? Y/N	Did you achieve it? Y/N
Write down your results (good or bad):	Write down your results (good or bad):
What was the difference in actual vs goal?	What was the difference in actual vs goal?
What actions or events contributed to these results?	What actions or events contributed to these results?
How does this affect your annual goal?	How does this affect your annual goal?
What would you do again or do diferently next time?	What would you do again or do diferently next time?

Monthly Action Planner

What do you want to complete or achieve this month? Take the time to plan out the tasks or actions you need to complete in order to successfully implement each strategy listed in your Quarterly Goals Planner.

Month:

TASKS	WEEK 1	WEEK 2	WEEK 3	WEEK 4

TASKS	WEEK 1	WEEK 2	WEEK 3	WEEK 4

Monthly Content Planner

Month:

	EMAIL NEWSLETTER TOPIC/OFFER:	BLOG TOPIC/OFFER:
WEEK 1:		
WEEK 2:		
WEEK 3:		
WEEK 4:		

Themes

FACEBOOK: INSTAGRAM: PINTEREST: YOUTUBE:

Month: 1 2 3 4 5 6 7 8 9 10 11 12

WEEK	MONDAY	TUESDAY	WEDNESDAY
THIS WEEK'S PRIORITIES			
THIS WEEK I WANT TO…			
WORK/BUSINESS TO-DOS			

THURSDAY	FRIDAY	SAT/SUN	WEEK IN REVIEW
			WINS
			REVENUE
			NUMBER OF ORDERS
			AVERAGE ORDER VALUE
			WEBSITE VISITORS/ LEADS
PERSONAL TO-DOS			CONVERSION RATE
			NEXT WEEK

127

Month: 1 2 3 4 5 6 7 8 9 10 11 12

WEEK	MONDAY	TUESDAY	WEDNESDAY
THIS WEEK'S PRIORITIES			

THIS WEEK I WANT TO…

WORK/BUSINESS TO-DOS

THURSDAY	FRIDAY	SAT/SUN	WEEK IN REVIEW
			WINS
			REVENUE
			NUMBER OF ORDERS
			AVERAGE ORDER VALUE
			WEBSITE VISITORS/ LEADS
PERSONAL TO-DOS			CONVERSION RATE
			NEXT WEEK

Month: 1 2 3 4 5 6 7 8 9 10 11 12

WEEK	MONDAY	TUESDAY	WEDNESDAY
THIS WEEK'S PRIORITIES			
THIS WEEK I WANT TO…			
WORK/BUSINESS TO-DOS			

THURSDAY	FRIDAY	SAT/SUN	WEEK IN REVIEW
			WINS
			REVENUE
			NUMBER OF ORDERS
			AVERAGE ORDER VALUE
			WEBSITE VISITORS/ LEADS
PERSONAL TO-DOS			CONVERSION RATE
			NEXT WEEK

Month: 1 2 3 4 5 6 7 8 9 10 11 12

WEEK	MONDAY	TUESDAY	WEDNESDAY
THIS WEEK'S PRIORITIES			

THIS WEEK I WANT TO…

WORK/BUSINESS TO-DOS

THURSDAY	FRIDAY	SAT/SUN	WEEK IN REVIEW
			WINS
			REVENUE
			NUMBER OF ORDERS
			AVERAGE ORDER VALUE
			WEBSITE VISITORS/ LEADS
PERSONAL TO-DOS			CONVERSION RATE
			NEXT WEEK

The monthly metrics

Website

OF VISITORS

OF ORDERS

$ OF SALES

CONVERSION RATE

OF NEW VISITORS

% BOUNCE RATE

FB Ads

OF VISITORS

OF ORDERS

$ OF SALES

CONVERSION RATE

ROAS

TOTAL SPEND

Emails

EMAILS SENT

OPEN RATE

OF ORDERS

$ OF SALES

CONVERSION RAT

Social Media

OF VISITORS

OF ORDERS

$ OF SALES

CONVERSION RATE

Other

OF VISITORS

OF ORDERS

$ OF SALES

CONVERSION RATE

MONTHLY SALES GOAL

MONTHLY SALES ACHIEVED

DIFFERENCE

What worked well this month

What didn't work well this month

Special occurrences during the month
(Ie Black Friday, Mother's Day, school holidays, product launch etc)

Monthly Action Planner

What do you want to complete or achieve this month? Take the time to plan out the tasks or actions you need to complete in order to successfully implement each strategy listed in your Quarterly Goals Planner.

Month:

TASKS	WEEK 1	WEEK 2	WEEK 3	WEEK 4

TASKS	WEEK 1	WEEK 2	WEEK 3	WEEK 4

Monthly Content Planner

Month:

	EMAIL NEWSLETTER TOPIC/OFFER:	BLOG TOPIC/OFFER:
WEEK 1:		
WEEK 2:		
WEEK 3:		
WEEK 4:		

Themes

FACEBOOK: INSTAGRAM: PINTEREST: YOUTUBE:

Month: 1 2 3 4 5 6 7 8 9 10 11 12

WEEK	MONDAY	TUESDAY	WEDNESDAY
THIS WEEK'S PRIORITIES			
THIS WEEK I WANT TO...			

WORK/BUSINESS TO-DOS

THURSDAY	FRIDAY	SAT/SUN	WEEK IN REVIEW
			WINS
			REVENUE
			NUMBER OF ORDERS
			AVERAGE ORDER VALUE
			WEBSITE VISITORS/ LEADS
PERSONAL TO-DOS			CONVERSION RATE
			NEXT WEEK

Month: 1 2 3 4 5 6 7 8 9 10 11 12

WEEK	MONDAY	TUESDAY	WEDNESDAY
THIS WEEK'S PRIORITIES			
THIS WEEK I WANT TO...			

WORK/BUSINESS TO-DOS

THURSDAY	FRIDAY	SAT/SUN	WEEK IN REVIEW
			WINS
			REVENUE
			NUMBER OF ORDERS
			AVERAGE ORDER VALUE
			WEBSITE VISITORS/ LEADS
PERSONAL TO-DOS			CONVERSION RATE
			NEXT WEEK

Month: 1 2 3 4 5 6 7 8 9 10 11 12

WEEK	MONDAY	TUESDAY	WEDNESDAY
THIS WEEK'S PRIORITIES			

THIS WEEK I WANT TO…

WORK/BUSINESS TO-DOS

THURSDAY	FRIDAY	SAT/SUN	WEEK IN REVIEW
			WINS
			REVENUE
			NUMBER OF ORDERS
			AVERAGE ORDER VALUE
			WEBSITE VISITORS/ LEADS
PERSONAL TO-DOS			CONVERSION RATE
			NEXT WEEK

Month: 1 2 3 4 5 6 7 8 9 10 11 12

WEEK	MONDAY	TUESDAY	WEDNESDAY
THIS WEEK'S PRIORITIES			
THIS WEEK I WANT TO...			
WORK/BUSINESS TO-DOS			

THURSDAY	FRIDAY	SAT/SUN	WEEK IN REVIEW
			WINS
			REVENUE
			NUMBER OF ORDERS
			AVERAGE ORDER VALUE
			WEBSITE VISITORS/ LEADS
PERSONAL TO-DOS			CONVERSION RATE
			NEXT WEEK

The monthly metrics

Website

OF VISITORS

OF ORDERS

$ OF SALES

CONVERSION RATE

OF NEW VISITORS

% BOUNCE RATE

FB Ads

OF VISITORS

OF ORDERS

$ OF SALES

CONVERSION RATE

ROAS

TOTAL SPEND

Emails

EMAILS SENT

OPEN RATE

OF ORDERS

$ OF SALES

CONVERSION RAT

Social Media

OF VISITORS

OF ORDERS

$ OF SALES

CONVERSION RATE

Other

OF VISITORS

OF ORDERS

$ OF SALES

CONVERSION RATE

MONTHLY SALES GOAL

MONTHLY SALES ACHIEVED

DIFFERENCE

What worked well this month

What didn't work well this month

Special occurrences during the month
(Ie Black Friday, Mother's Day, school holidays, product launch etc)

Monthly Action Planner

What do you want to complete or achieve this month? Take the time to plan out the tasks or actions you need to complete in order to successfully implement each strategy listed in your Quarterly Goals Planner.

Month:

TASKS	WEEK 1	WEEK 2	WEEK 3	WEEK 4

TASKS	WEEK 1	WEEK 2	WEEK 3	WEEK 4

Monthly Content Planner

Month:

	EMAIL NEWSLETTER TOPIC/OFFER:	BLOG TOPIC/OFFER:
WEEK 1:		
WEEK 2:		
WEEK 3:		
WEEK 4:		

Themes

FACEBOOK: INSTAGRAM: PINTEREST: YOUTUBE:

Month: 1 2 3 4 5 6 7 8 9 10 11 12

WEEK	MONDAY	TUESDAY	WEDNESDAY
THIS WEEK'S PRIORITIES			
THIS WEEK I WANT TO…			
WORK/BUSINESS TO-DOS			

THURSDAY	FRIDAY	SAT/SUN	WEEK IN REVIEW
			WINS
			REVENUE
			NUMBER OF ORDERS
			AVERAGE ORDER VALUE
			WEBSITE VISITORS/ LEADS
PERSONAL TO-DOS			CONVERSION RATE
			NEXT WEEK

Month: 1 2 3 4 5 6 7 8 9 10 11 12

WEEK	MONDAY	TUESDAY	WEDNESDAY
THIS WEEK'S PRIORITIES			
THIS WEEK I WANT TO...			
WORK/BUSINESS TO-DOS			

THURSDAY	FRIDAY	SAT/SUN	WEEK IN REVIEW
			WINS
			REVENUE
			NUMBER OF ORDERS
			AVERAGE ORDER VALUE
			WEBSITE VISITORS/ LEADS
PERSONAL TO-DOS			CONVERSION RATE
			NEXT WEEK

Month: 1 2 3 4 5 6 7 8 9 10 11 12

WEEK	MONDAY	TUESDAY	WEDNESDAY
THIS WEEK'S PRIORITIES			
THIS WEEK I WANT TO…			
WORK/BUSINESS TO-DOS			

THURSDAY	FRIDAY	SAT/SUN	WEEK IN REVIEW
			WINS
			REVENUE
			NUMBER OF ORDERS
			AVERAGE ORDER VALUE
			WEBSITE VISITORS/ LEADS
PERSONAL TO-DOS			CONVERSION RATE
			NEXT WEEK

Month: 1 2 3 4 5 6 7 8 9 10 11 12

WEEK	MONDAY	TUESDAY	WEDNESDAY

THIS WEEK'S
PRIORITIES

THIS WEEK I WANT
TO...

WORK/BUSINESS TO-DOS

THURSDAY	FRIDAY	SAT/SUN	WEEK IN REVIEW
			WINS
			REVENUE
			NUMBER OF ORDERS
			AVERAGE ORDER VALUE
			WEBSITE VISITORS/ LEADS
PERSONAL TO-DOS			CONVERSION RATE
			NEXT WEEK

The monthly metrics

Website

OF VISITORS

OF ORDERS

$ OF SALES

CONVERSION RATE

OF NEW VISITORS

% BOUNCE RATE

FB Ads

OF VISITORS

OF ORDERS

$ OF SALES

CONVERSION RATE

ROAS

TOTAL SPEND

Emails

EMAILS SENT

OPEN RATE

OF ORDERS

$ OF SALES

CONVERSION RAT

Social Media

OF VISITORS

OF ORDERS

$ OF SALES

CONVERSION RATE

Other

OF VISITORS

OF ORDERS

$ OF SALES

CONVERSION RATE

MONTHLY SALES GOAL

MONTHLY SALES ACHIEVED

DIFFERENCE

What worked well this month

What didn't work well this month

Special occurrences during the month
(Ie Black Friday, Mother's Day, school holidays, product launch etc)

Quarterly Goal Review

If there was one thing you could do to significantly increase your chances of successfully achieving your goals, would you do it?

Yes? Great! Because here it is: **Take the time every 90 days to review your progress.**

QUARTERLY GOAL 1:

What was your goal?

Did you achieve it? Y/N

Write down your results (good or bad):

What was the difference in actual vs goal?

What actions or events contributed to these results?

How does this affect your annual goal?

What would you do again or do diferently next time?

QUARTERLY GOAL 2:

What was your goal?

Did you achieve it? Y/N

Write down your results (good or bad):

What was the difference in actual vs goal?

What actions or events contributed to these results?

How does this affect your annual goal?

What would you do again or do diferently next time?

By monitoring and reviewing your progress, you will see how much you've achieved already, and this can have a powerful psychological impact on how motivated and positive you feel. Give yourself an hour to review your goals using the following worksheet as a guide.

Go back to the goals you made for the Year and the Quarter and enter them here to see how you are tracking.

QUARTERLY GOAL 3:

What was your goal?

Did you achieve it? Y/N

Write down your results (good or bad):

What was the difference in actual vs goal?

What actions or events contributed to these results?

How does this affect your annual goal?

What would you do again or do diferently next time?

QUARTERLY GOAL 4:

What was your goal?

Did you achieve it? Y/N

Write down your results (good or bad):

What was the difference in actual vs goal?

What actions or events contributed to these results?

How does this affect your annual goal?

What would you do again or do diferently next time?

Enjoy feeling organised?

Don't forget to order
your next year's

PRODUCTPRENEUR
SUCCESS PLANNER!!

Head to

www.catherinelangman.com today.

Monthly Action Planner

What do you want to complete or achieve this month? Take the time to plan out the tasks or actions you need to complete in order to successfully implement each strategy listed in your Quarterly Goals Planner.

Month:

TASKS	WEEK 1	WEEK 2	WEEK 3	WEEK 4

TASKS	WEEK 1	WEEK 2	WEEK 3	WEEK 4

Monthly Content Planner

Month:

	EMAIL NEWSLETTER TOPIC/OFFER:	BLOG TOPIC/OFFER:
WEEK 1:		
WEEK 2:		
WEEK 3:		
WEEK 4:		

Themes

FACEBOOK: INSTAGRAM: PINTEREST: YOUTUBE:

Month: 1 2 3 4 5 6 7 8 9 10 11 12

WEEK	MONDAY	TUESDAY	WEDNESDAY
THIS WEEK'S PRIORITIES			
THIS WEEK I WANT TO…			

WORK/BUSINESS TO-DOS

THURSDAY	FRIDAY	SAT/SUN	WEEK IN REVIEW
			WINS
			REVENUE
			NUMBER OF ORDERS
			AVERAGE ORDER VALUE
			WEBSITE VISITORS/ LEADS
PERSONAL TO-DOS			CONVERSION RATE
			NEXT WEEK

Month: 1   2   3   4   5   6   7   8   9   10   11   12

WEEK	MONDAY	TUESDAY	WEDNESDAY
THIS WEEK'S PRIORITIES			
THIS WEEK I WANT TO…			
WORK/BUSINESS TO-DOS			

THURSDAY	FRIDAY	SAT/SUN	WEEK IN REVIEW
			WINS
			REVENUE
			NUMBER OF ORDERS
			AVERAGE ORDER VALUE
			WEBSITE VISITORS/ LEADS
PERSONAL TO-DOS			CONVERSION RATE
			NEXT WEEK

Month: 1 2 3 4 5 6 7 8 9 10 11 12

WEEK	MONDAY	TUESDAY	WEDNESDAY
THIS WEEK'S PRIORITIES			
THIS WEEK I WANT TO...			

WORK/BUSINESS TO-DOS

THURSDAY	FRIDAY	SAT/SUN	WEEK IN REVIEW
			WINS
			REVENUE
			NUMBER OF ORDERS
			AVERAGE ORDER VALUE
			WEBSITE VISITORS/ LEADS
PERSONAL TO-DOS			CONVERSION RATE
			NEXT WEEK

Month: 1 2 3 4 5 6 7 8 9 10 11 12

WEEK	MONDAY	TUESDAY	WEDNESDAY
THIS WEEK'S PRIORITIES			
THIS WEEK I WANT TO…			
WORK/BUSINESS TO-DOS			

THURSDAY	FRIDAY	SAT/SUN	WEEK IN REVIEW
			WINS
			REVENUE
			NUMBER OF ORDERS
			AVERAGE ORDER VALUE
			WEBSITE VISITORS/ LEADS
PERSONAL TO-DOS			CONVERSION RATE
			NEXT WEEK

The monthly metrics

Website

OF VISITORS

OF ORDERS

$ OF SALES

CONVERSION RATE

OF NEW VISITORS

% BOUNCE RATE

FB Ads

OF VISITORS

OF ORDERS

$ OF SALES

CONVERSION RATE

ROAS

TOTAL SPEND

Emails

EMAILS SENT

OPEN RATE

OF ORDERS

$ OF SALES

CONVERSION RAT

Social Media

OF VISITORS

OF ORDERS

$ OF SALES

CONVERSION RATE

Other

OF VISITORS

OF ORDERS

$ OF SALES

CONVERSION RATE

MONTHLY SALES GOAL

MONTHLY SALES ACHIEVED

DIFFERENCE

What worked well this month

What didn't work well this month

Special occurrences during the month
(Ie Black Friday, Mother's Day, school holidays, product launch etc)

Monthly Action Planner

What do you want to complete or achieve this month? Take the time to plan out the tasks or actions you need to complete in order to successfully implement each strategy listed in your Quarterly Goals Planner.

Month:

TASKS	WEEK 1	WEEK 2	WEEK 3	WEEK 4

TASKS	WEEK 1	WEEK 2	WEEK 3	WEEK 4

Monthly Content Planner

Month:

	EMAIL NEWSLETTER TOPIC/OFFER:	BLOG TOPIC/OFFER:
WEEK 1:		
WEEK 2:		
WEEK 3:		
WEEK 4:		

Themes

FACEBOOK: INSTAGRAM: PINTEREST: YOUTUBE:

Month: 1 2 3 4 5 6 7 8 9 10 11 12

WEEK	MONDAY	TUESDAY	WEDNESDAY
THIS WEEK'S PRIORITIES			
THIS WEEK I WANT TO…			

WORK/BUSINESS TO-DOS

THURSDAY	FRIDAY	SAT/SUN	WEEK IN REVIEW
			WINS
			REVENUE
			NUMBER OF ORDERS
			AVERAGE ORDER VALUE
			WEBSITE VISITORS/ LEADS
PERSONAL TO-DOS			CONVERSION RATE
			NEXT WEEK

Month: 1 2 3 4 5 6 7 8 9 10 11 12

WEEK	MONDAY	TUESDAY	WEDNESDAY
THIS WEEK'S PRIORITIES			

THIS WEEK I WANT TO...

WORK/BUSINESS TO-DOS

THURSDAY	FRIDAY	SAT/SUN	WEEK IN REVIEW
			WINS
			REVENUE
			NUMBER OF ORDERS
			AVERAGE ORDER VALUE
			WEBSITE VISITORS/ LEADS
PERSONAL TO-DOS			CONVERSION RATE
			NEXT WEEK

Month: 1 2 3 4 5 6 7 8 9 10 11 12

WEEK	MONDAY	TUESDAY	WEDNESDAY
THIS WEEK'S PRIORITIES			
THIS WEEK I WANT TO...			
WORK/BUSINESS TO-DOS			

THURSDAY	FRIDAY	SAT/SUN	WEEK IN REVIEW
			WINS
			REVENUE
			NUMBER OF ORDERS
			AVERAGE ORDER VALUE
			WEBSITE VISITORS/ LEADS
PERSONAL TO-DOS			CONVERSION RATE
			NEXT WEEK

Month: 1 2 3 4 5 6 7 8 9 10 11 12

WEEK	MONDAY	TUESDAY	WEDNESDAY
THIS WEEK'S PRIORITIES			

THIS WEEK I WANT TO...

WORK/BUSINESS TO-DOS

THURSDAY	FRIDAY	SAT/SUN	WEEK IN REVIEW
			WINS
			REVENUE
			NUMBER OF ORDERS
			AVERAGE ORDER VALUE
			WEBSITE VISITORS/ LEADS
PERSONAL TO-DOS			CONVERSION RATE
			NEXT WEEK

The monthly metrics

Website

OF VISITORS

OF ORDERS

$ OF SALES

CONVERSION RATE

OF NEW VISITORS

% BOUNCE RATE

FB Ads

OF VISITORS

OF ORDERS

$ OF SALES

CONVERSION RATE

ROAS

TOTAL SPEND

Emails

EMAILS SENT

OPEN RATE

OF ORDERS

$ OF SALES

CONVERSION RAT

Social Media

OF VISITORS

OF ORDERS

$ OF SALES

CONVERSION RATE

Other

OF VISITORS

OF ORDERS

$ OF SALES

CONVERSION RATE

MONTHLY SALES GOAL

MONTHLY SALES ACHIEVED

DIFFERENCE

What worked well this month

What didn't work well this month

Special occurrences during the month
(Ie Black Friday, Mother's Day, school holidays, product launch etc)

Monthly Action Planner

What do you want to complete or achieve this month? Take the time to plan out the tasks or actions you need to complete in order to successfully implement each strategy listed in your Quarterly Goals Planner.

Month:

TASKS	WEEK 1	WEEK 2	WEEK 3	WEEK 4

TASKS	WEEK 1	WEEK 2	WEEK 3	WEEK 4

Monthly Content Planner

Month:

	EMAIL NEWSLETTER TOPIC/OFFER:	BLOG TOPIC/OFFER:
WEEK 1:		
WEEK 2:		
WEEK 3:		
WEEK 4:		

Themes

FACEBOOK: INSTAGRAM: PINTEREST: YOUTUBE:

Month: 1 2 3 4 5 6 7 8 9 10 11 12

WEEK	MONDAY	TUESDAY	WEDNESDAY
THIS WEEK'S PRIORITIES			
THIS WEEK I WANT TO…			
WORK/BUSINESS TO-DOS			

THURSDAY	FRIDAY	SAT/SUN	WEEK IN REVIEW
			WINS
			REVENUE
			NUMBER OF ORDERS
			AVERAGE ORDER VALUE
			WEBSITE VISITORS/ LEADS
PERSONAL TO-DOS			CONVERSION RATE
			NEXT WEEK

Month: 1 2 3 4 5 6 7 8 9 10 11 12

WEEK	MONDAY	TUESDAY	WEDNESDAY
THIS WEEK'S PRIORITIES			
THIS WEEK I WANT TO…			
WORK/BUSINESS TO-DOS			

THURSDAY	FRIDAY	SAT/SUN	WEEK IN REVIEW
			WINS
			REVENUE
			NUMBER OF ORDERS
			AVERAGE ORDER VALUE
			WEBSITE VISITORS/ LEADS
PERSONAL TO-DOS			CONVERSION RATE
			NEXT WEEK

Month: 1 2 3 4 5 6 7 8 9 10 11 12

WEEK	MONDAY	TUESDAY	WEDNESDAY
THIS WEEK'S PRIORITIES			
THIS WEEK I WANT TO...			

WORK/BUSINESS TO-DOS

THURSDAY	FRIDAY	SAT/SUN	WEEK IN REVIEW
			WINS
			REVENUE
			NUMBER OF ORDERS
			AVERAGE ORDER VALUE
			WEBSITE VISITORS/ LEADS
PERSONAL TO-DOS			CONVERSION RATE
			NEXT WEEK

Month: 1 2 3 4 5 6 7 8 9 10 11 12

WEEK	MONDAY	TUESDAY	WEDNESDAY
THIS WEEK'S PRIORITIES			

THIS WEEK I WANT TO…

WORK/BUSINESS TO-DOS

THURSDAY	FRIDAY	SAT/SUN	WEEK IN REVIEW
			WINS
			REVENUE
			NUMBER OF ORDERS
			AVERAGE ORDER VALUE
			WEBSITE VISITORS/ LEADS
PERSONAL TO-DOS			CONVERSION RATE
			NEXT WEEK

The monthly metrics

Website

OF VISITORS

OF ORDERS

$ OF SALES

CONVERSION RATE

OF NEW VISITORS

% BOUNCE RATE

FB Ads

OF VISITORS

OF ORDERS

$ OF SALES

CONVERSION RATE

ROAS

TOTAL SPEND

Emails

EMAILS SENT

OPEN RATE

OF ORDERS

$ OF SALES

CONVERSION RAT

Social Media

OF VISITORS

OF ORDERS

$ OF SALES

CONVERSION RATE

Other

OF VISITORS

OF ORDERS

$ OF SALES

CONVERSION RATE

MONTHLY SALES GOAL

MONTHLY SALES ACHIEVED

DIFFERENCE

What worked well this month

What didn't work well this month

Special occurrences during the month
(Ie Black Friday, Mother's Day, school holidays, product launch etc)

Quarterly Goal Review

If there was one thing you could do to significantly increase your chances of successfully achieving your goals, would you do it?

Yes? Great! Because here it is: **Take the time every 90 days to review your progress.**

QUARTERLY GOAL 1:

What was your goal?

Did you achieve it? Y/N

Write down your results (good or bad):

What was the difference in actual vs goal?

What actions or events contributed to these results?

How does this affect your annual goal?

What would you do again or do diferently next time?

QUARTERLY GOAL 2:

What was your goal?

Did you achieve it? Y/N

Write down your results (good or bad):

What was the difference in actual vs goal?

What actions or events contributed to these results?

How does this affect your annual goal?

What would you do again or do diferently next time?

By monitoring and reviewing your progress, you will see how much you've achieved already, and this can have a powerful psychological impact on how motivated and positive you feel. Give yourself an hour to review your goals using the following worksheet as a guide.

Go back to the goals you made for the Year and the Quarter and enter them here to see how you are tracking.

QUARTERLY GOAL 3:	QUARTERLY GOAL 4:
What was your goal?	What was your goal?
Did you achieve it? Y/N	Did you achieve it? Y/N
Write down your results (good or bad):	Write down your results (good or bad):
What was the difference in actual vs goal?	What was the difference in actual vs goal?
What actions or events contributed to these results?	What actions or events contributed to these results?
How does this affect your annual goal?	How does this affect your annual goal?
What would you do again or do diferently next time?	What would you do again or do diferently next time?

Contact list

GRAPHIC DESIGNER	
MANUFACTURERS	
AGENT	
VA	
WEB DEVELOPER	
PR	
STAFF	
COACH	
PRINTER	
COURIER	

Contact list

GRAPHIC DESIGNER	
MANUFACTURERS	
AGENT	
VA	
WEB DEVELOPER	
PR	
STAFF	
COACH	
PRINTER	
COURIER	

Your notes

National Library of Australia Cataloguing-in-Publication data:
The Productpreneur Success Planner/KMD Press

Interior designer: Ida Jansson

ISBN 978-0-6486984-1-8

www.ingramcontent.com/pod-product-compliance
Lightning Source LLC
Chambersburg PA
CBHW051928190326
41458CB00026B/6443